She Persisted

HARRIET TUBMAN

— INSPIRED BY —

She Persisted

by Chelsea Clinton & Alexandra Boiger

······································

HARRIET TUBMAN

······································

Written by
Andrea Davis Pinkney

Interior illustrations by
Gillian Flint

PHILOMEL

PHILOMEL BOOKS
An imprint of Penguin Random House LLC, New York

First published in the United States of America by Philomel,
an imprint of Penguin Random House LLC, 2021.

Text copyright © 2021 by Chelsea Clinton.
Illustrations copyright © 2021 by Alexandra Boiger.

Visit us online at penguinrandomhouse.com.

Library of Congress Cataloging-in-Publication Data is available.

Printed in the United States of America

HC ISBN 9780593115657
PB ISBN 9780593115664

10 9 8 7 6 5 4 3 2 1

Edited by Jill Santopolo.
Design by Ellice M. Lee.
Text set in LTC Kennerley.

For

Gwennie, Lynne and Taryn

She
Persisted

....

DEAR READER,

As Sally Ride and Marian Wright Edelman both powerfully
said, "You can't be what you can't see." When Sally Ride said
that, she meant that it was hard to dream of being an astronaut,
like she was, or a doctor or an athlete or anything at all if you
didn't see someone like you who already had lived that dream.
She especially was talking about seeing women in jobs that
historically were held by men.

I wrote the first *She Persisted* and the books that came
after it because I wanted young girls—and children of all
genders—to see women who worked hard to live their dreams.
And I wanted all of us to see examples of persistence in the face
of different challenges to help inspire us in our own lives.

I'm so thrilled now to partner with a sisterhood of
writers to bring longer, more in-depth versions of these stories
of women's persistence and achievement to readers. I hope
you enjoy these chapter books as much as I do and find them
inspiring and empowering.

And remember: If anyone ever tells you no, if anyone
ever says your voice isn't important or your dreams are too big,
remember these women. They persisted and so should you.

Warmly,

Chelsea Clinton

HARRIET TUBMAN

TABLE OF CONTENTS

....

CHAPTER I

Bright-Eyed Girl

When Harriet Green gave birth to her daughter, she held that baby close, whispered a sweet hello, and loved the child with all her heart. The newborn's father, Benjamin Ross, most likely cradled his tiny daughter. He was as proud as any daddy could be.

The baby was born on a night so dark, you couldn't see past its black. But the light in that child's eyes was brighter than bright. She had a twinkle about her that shone like the sky's prettiest stars.

Nobody knows the exact date this bright-eyed girl came into the world. She was born at a time when not everyone recorded birthdays. It was sometime between 1820 and 1822. Though no one remembers the precise year, one thing's for certain: this girl grew up to become a great lady whose bravery and grit persisted her whole life, and inspired others to follow.

Harriet and Benjamin went by the nicknames Old Rit and Old Ben. Their new baby daughter was one of nine children. They gave her two names. Harriet, after her mother, and Araminta, which means prayer and protection. Folks called the child Minty for short.

When Minty was born, she cried loudly. It was as if she was shouting her arrival, letting everyone know she had been born to do great things. The North Star's glistening light kept watch over Minty. That star would be a guiding presence for her entire life. It never lost sight of what was beautiful about her.

Old Rit and Old Ben lived on the Edward Brodess planation in Dorchester County, Maryland. As enslaved people, they were owned by the Brodess family. Minty and her parents were considered property, in the same way people had objects like a tea kettle or a hammer that belonged to them. That's what slavery was—White people owning Black people. The Black people worked without pay, and had to do whatever they were told. They called their owners "Master" or "Mistress" because these men and women ruled their lives. And, just like objects, enslaved people could be bought, sold, or traded. It didn't matter how old you were, or if you were a man, woman, or child. Mothers and fathers could be sold away from their children, and kids could be purchased and forced to leave their parents.

Sometimes members of a family were split up and sold away from each other without warning. A master or mistress would call you over, look you in the eye, and tell you it was time to say goodbye to those you loved the most.

This is one of the reasons life for enslaved people was so frightening and uncertain. But one thing was for sure: enslaved people were *not* things. They were human beings with dignity, self-respect and intelligence. These smart, determined people took pride in themselves and their work. They built strong families whose love kept them going through hard times, and whose faith grew as they built a legacy of courage.

Faith and love lived deep in the hearts of Old Rit and Old Ben. They passed these virtues on to Minty.

As she grew, Minty had it hard. Master Brodess was as mean as they come, and greedier than ten hungry hogs. To make money, he *rented* Minty to the Cook family, farmers who lived near marshy wetlands. Like Master Brodess, the Cooks were cruel people. Minty was only six or seven years old, when she was forced to wade into icy water to catch muskrats snagged in Master Cook's riverbank traps.

Whew, that water was *freezing*. One day, Minty caught a cold, got a fever and got the measles, all at once. To Master Cook's way of thinking, his "rented" child was now a bad investment. He sent her back to Brodess land. Minty soon discovered that she needed what her full name, Araminta, had promised—prayer and protection.

CHAPTER 2

The North Star's Diamond Light

As soon as Old Rit nursed little Minty back to health, Master Brodess rented her out again to a lady needing help with her baby. Minty had to call this woman Mistress.

Snagging muskrats was miserable work, but changing smelly diapers and keeping a fussy baby from crying took just as much care and attention. Minty could never take her eye off that baby. To make matters worse, Mistress always seemed to have *her* eye on Minty, watching every move she made.

One morning, while tending to the baby, Minty's mind started to wander. She couldn't help but notice a bowl of sugar lumps resting on the table nearby. Those crystal lumps caught glints of the sun. It was as if they were winking at Minty and whispering her name. For a quick moment, when Mistress wasn't looking, Minty secretly slipped a sugar lump onto her tongue. She had never tasted sugar before that day. Oh, the sweetness! That glimmering crystal melting in Minty's mouth eased some of the bitterness she had suffered. But when Mistress caught Minty savoring this delicious treat, the sweet taste of escaping such hard work turned sour in a snap. Mistress came after Minty with a whip made of tough animal skin.

Minty ran and ran, till she'd outrun Mistress. Her heart pumped a sure rhythm in her chest. The flutter of freedom beat like the wings of a boundless bird, flying away from her cruel mistress!

Working hard to catch her breath, Minty settled into a pigpen, where a sow lived with her piglets. Minty hid there for nearly a week. Later in

her life, when she looked back on that time, she said, "I didn't have anywhere else to go, even though I knew what was coming."

That pigpen was hot and stinky, and the sow was as mean as any mistress. Minty had to fight off the mama pig, wrestling her for food scraps. Minty got so tired and hungry that she crawled back to Mistress, who whipped Minty with the rawhide switch, then returned her to the Brodess planta-tion, complaining that she was a bad purchase. As soon as Old Rit took a look at her little girl, she hugged her, tenderly dressed her wounds, and sang her to sleep each night.

While running from Mistress with the whip, Minty felt freedom's power in her feet. And now that she'd tasted sugar's sweetness, she had a hunger for what was possible. Minty had experienced what fleeing could mean, even though it was brief.

To get free, an enslaved person had to make it from the southern part of America to certain states in the North where slavery had come to an end. In many Northern states, Black people still faced unfair treatment, but they weren't owned by anyone, and earned money for the work they did.

But escaping from slavery was dangerous. It meant risking being caught by a master or some other White man on the lookout for runaways. The stories about what happened if you were found while trying to escape stopped a lot of people from running away. These stories were scary, and true. If you were caught while traveling up North, you could be beaten with the same whip they used to punish a horse. Or, even worse, you could be sold away from your family, never to see them again. These stories didn't stop Minty. She was determined to get free, and to help others make it to freedom, too.

One night Old Ben showed Minty the North Star, a twinkling diamond on the sky's

black cape that pointed north. Following the North Star led to freedom. It looked like the same star that had greeted Minty on the night she was born.

....

CHAPTER 3

Dreams of Freedom

When Minty was a teenager, she was still working on the Brodess plantation, hauling heaps of hay, picking prickly cotton that brought blisters to her skin, washing the master's dirty underpants, peeling onions and doing any other labor her owners demanded. Her days started as soon as the sun rose, and didn't end until long after that same sun, tired from *its* hard work, set for the night.

Sometime around 1835, Minty was hired by a man named Barrett. Her job was to work the crops to be harvested. One day, while tending to her duties, she noticed a Black man named Robert, one of Barrett's enslaved workers, leaving the fields without permission. The overseer, the boss whose job it was to watch the workers, spotted Robert and followed him. Minty was close behind. She was curious to see if Robert was trying to get free, and how he would do it. Robert had only made it to the town store when the overseer caught up to him, pulled out a whip and raised it high. He was good and ready to beat Robert.

Before the overseer flung his whip to Robert's back, Minty blocked him so Robert could run. And run he did, with Minty close behind. The overseer grabbed a lead weight, hurling it at the

man. It missed the runaway, but instead—*bam!*—hit Minty in the forehead!

She bled and bled. And cried and cried. And prayed and prayed she wouldn't die. Old Rit and Old Ben prayed too, as they nursed their daughter back to health again. Minty fell into a coma, a long sleep that never seemed to end. She stayed unconscious through the long, dark winter. Come spring, Minty's coma ended. Flowers and trees started to bloom. So did Minty's strength. The wound from the lead weight had left a dent in her forehead. Its puckered scar made Minty more committed than ever to do what it took to gain her freedom.

Minty's injury had brought on a sickness that folks called "the sleeping disease." It was a problem that would stay with Minty her whole life. Anytime, anywhere, with no warning, Minty could fall into a deep sleep, and not wake up until the sleeping spell wore off. It could last a few hours, a whole day, or longer. To make matters worse, Minty had to put up with pounding headaches. Master Brodess showed no sympathy. To him, Minty was now damaged property, and he was eager to sell her to anyone who'd pay a decent price. But nobody wanted to purchase a worker who could fall asleep at any moment.

In 1844 Minty found a bit of happiness when

she married John Tubman, a free Black man who had never been enslaved. She took John's last name. And it was around this time that Minty told people to call her Harriet, to honor her mother.

But Harriet's joy didn't last long. Even though John was free, Harriet was still enslaved, by law. Soon, John started to turn on Harriet, treating her like she was *his* slave.

Harriet would not allow her husband to crush her spirit. It was bad enough that she was owned by the Brodess family, but now the man she married was acting like her master. Not only did he insist that Harriet wash, cook and clean for him, he did not like how outspoken his wife was becoming. Harriet was beginning to voice her opinions about the ugly ways of slavery and how much she disliked John's way of making her feel small by demanding that she work for him.

Whenever Harriet got to talking about escaping to freedom, John was quick to stomp down on her dream. He threatened his wife by letting her know that he'd go straight to Master Brodess and tell on her if she ran away.

That's when Harriet Tubman made an important decision. She would keep her longing for freedom locked deep inside her heart, where John couldn't reach it.

When Harriet and John had been married for about five years, Master Brodess called everyone together on his property to share a heap of bad news. He'd fallen deep into debt. The only way he could save himself from ruin would be to sell the men and women who he owned as his slaves.

The first to be sold were two of Harriet's

sisters. Master Brodess's overseer put chains on each one, and sent them to separate locations in what was known as "cotton country," the southernmost states where the grizzliest masters lived, and where enslaved people feared they'd be forced to go. Cotton country got its name from the abundance of cotton crops that grew in that region.

With her beloved sisters gone, Harriet was more focused than ever on making her dream of freedom come true for herself and others.

······························

Bound for the Promised Land

Word among enslaved people traveled through the whispering lips of *did-you-know-did-you-hear*. Folks got information from one person telling another, who then passed it on to the next, until news had quietly reached many.

That's how Harriet learned about abolitionists, women and men who were working to end slavery. These were Black and White people who had created a system for hiding runaways who were making their way to freedom.

The *did-you-know-did-you-hear* whispers turned into a network of *hide-and-help* that people called the Underground Railroad. The railroad wasn't made of iron cars. No smokestacks or choo-choo trains. No cross-tie tracks.

This railroad was navigated using stars to lead the way in the blackest night. *This* railroad was built by kind folks helping to hide enslaved people who were seeking freedom.

The Underground Railroad's engine was fueled by heartbeats and dreams, chugging toward change. Its passengers were enslaved people sleeping under burlap sacks. Hiding in salt shacks, keeping their souls' hope alive. The Underground Railroad's powerful engine of people helping people was like a quiet storm that came through the whispers of generous folks saying, *Together we can!*

Word spread that a White woman who lived near to the Brodess plantation was helping runaways use the Underground Railroad. And when folks talked, Harriet listened. But she never spoke about it to her husband, John.

One night, while John was asleep, Harriet showed the North Star to two of her brothers, and

encouraged them to escape with her. They agreed, and the three of them set out silently. Not long into their journey, Harriet's brothers got scared. They refused to keep going. They made Harriet come back with them to the planation.

Two days passed. Harriet couldn't help but wonder if she'd missed her opportunity to flee by returning with her brothers. But when Harriet heard rumors that she was about to be sold and sent to cotton country, her resolve became even stronger. She *resisted* being sold by immediately making a plan to flee. Within herself, she *insisted* that the time had truly come to get gone. She *persisted* in holding fast to her dream of freedom.

Harriet had to keep her determination a secret. To do this, she spoke in code. This was something many enslaved people did. By singing spirituals while they worked, they secretly let others know they were planning an escape. The words of these songs were their way of saying goodbye:

> When that old chariot comes,
> I'm going to leave you.
> I'm bound for the promised land.
> Friends, I'm going to leave you.

And that's just what Harriet did. She packed a small croker sack with salted pork, bread and corn pone, and snuck away to the home of the White woman who was part of the Underground Railroad's network. The woman, who was a Quaker, helped Harriet find another woman whose husband could drive her farther north in his carriage.

When Harriet arrived at the next house, the woman who lived there thrust a broom into Harriet's hands and insisted that she start sweeping. This frightened Harriet. She worried that an evil trick had been played on her. Harriet was afraid she'd been caught, and would be sent back to slavery. But these people were on Harriet's side. The sweeping *was* a trick, but not on Harriet. Having her appear to be busily working, as if she was the lady's slave, was their way of fooling any White folks who were on the hunt for escaping Black people.

The trick worked. Later, after the sun set, and the North Star rose high, the lady's husband tucked Harriet in the bed of his wagon under a heap of blankets. He piled burlap potato sacks on top. Harriet was hidden real good. As the carriage bumped and rolled on the dirt road, Harriet kept very still. This was her first trip on the Underground Railroad. It lasted all night.

When dawn came, the man told Harriet the route to take that would lead her to freedom over the days ahead. The trip was not easy. Harriet had to travel on foot through wet, marshy soil. She was forced to put up with biting mosquitoes and thorny bushes that poked at her skin. Harriet also faced cold nights and a growling stomach. She'd eaten everything packed in her croker sack. The Underground Railroad helpers had also given her food to carry, but the supply was running low. Harriet soon had to live on whatever berries or other natural foods she could find in the woods.

With determination churning like a furnace, Harriet ran and ran with all her might up the

Eastern Shore toward Pennsylvania, nearly ninety miles from Master Brodess's plantation. Her owner had most likely sent bloodhounds and a group of searchers to look for her. The scar on her forehead was a way to identify who she was. As a disguise, Harriet sometimes pulled a man's hat down low on her head, or wore the veil of an elegant lady to cover her scar. This kept her safe. Harriet still struggled with her sleeping disease and the headaches it caused. Knowing she could fall asleep at any moment was scary. But fear never stopped Harriet, and the disease never got in the way of her progress.

Exhausted and excited, Harriet finally reached Pennsylvania, which was a free state. It was a morning in 1849. The sky rolled out like a glistening piecrust to greet her. Years later, when Harriet recalled that special moment, she said, "I looked at my hands to see if I was the same person, now that I was *free*. There was such glory over everything. The sun came like gold through the trees and over the fields, and I felt like I was in Heaven."

CHAPTER 5

The Woman Called Moses

Harriet couldn't fully enjoy her freedom while her family still suffered under the weight of slavery. She often thought about Old Rit, Old Ben and her sisters and brothers. And she missed them. Years later, when Harriet was reflecting on that time in her life, she said, "I was free, but there was no one to welcome me to the land of freedom. I was a stranger in a strange land."

Harriet's family was in Maryland, continuing

the backbreaking work enslaved people were forced to endure. Harriet vowed to somehow help them get to freedom. It was one thing to escape alone, only having to hide herself and be accountable for her own care. But helping groups of people find freedom was a much greater responsibility.

Harriet wondered how she could take on something so big, and so hard. Being a woman of faith, Harriet prayed. "Oh, dear Lord," she said, "I ain't got no friend but you. Come to my help, Lord, for I'm in trouble."

Harriet Tubman didn't shy back from trouble. She was good at meeting challenges face-on. And that's just what she did. She got a job in Philadelphia, cooking and cleaning in a hotel's kitchen. Harriet's work days were long, strenuous and boring. But for the first time in her life, she was earning money.

This was not slave labor. Harriet was now a working woman who took pride in the wages she made and the cash she was able to save.

Harriet found out about an organization called the Philadelphia Vigilance Committee, a group of women and men who helped enslaved people escape along the Underground Railroad. The committee's leaders were James Miller McKim, a White minister, and William Still, a Black man who'd been born free in Philadelphia. Harriet and William got to be friends. William introduced Harriet to people who, like her, had successfully escaped to freedom. These folks shared their stories, and gave Harriet details about the routes and methods they'd used to run away without being caught.

Members of the Philadelphia Vigilance Committee formed a very strong network of

did-you-know-did-you-hear. They had lots of information about the doings down south. They let Harriet know that her niece, Kessiah, was about to be sold and sent to cotton country. Harriet immediately made a plan to return to Maryland to get her niece and bring her to freedom before it was too late.

Kessiah's husband, John Bowley, was a free Black man. By making connections through the kindhearted people along the Underground Railroad, he came up with a way of getting Kessiah and their two children to Baltimore, Maryland. But once they arrived in Baltimore, they would need a strong, brave person to help transport them safely from Baltimore to Pennsylvania—to freedom.

Harriet didn't have to think twice about what to do. She was more than ready to guide her family members to free land. William Still urged Harriet not to risk her own freedom and safety by helping others. William told Harriet it was too dangerous. Well, *she* told *him* that rescuing her niece wasn't up for debate.

When Kessiah, John and their children arrived in Baltimore, Harriet was there to greet them. Like other escapes, this one wasn't easy. Harriet was now traveling with kids who had to stay awake during the night's darkest hours so they could keep moving forward toward freedom with the rest of the group. When it rained, they traveled in wet clothes that stuck to their skin. Blisters formed on their feet from walking so many miles. When a shiver or cough came on, sometimes they ignored it. There was no time to waste, even if someone got sick. Harriet and her family kept their spirits up by singing and praying together.

After uncertain days and nights of travel, Harriet got her family safely to Philadelphia. This rescue encouraged Harriet to help even more people, which she did. In 1851, she rescued her brother Moses and several others, guiding them through dark nights and frightening times, but always transporting them to the sunlight of liber-ation that shone through dark clouds once they'd reached free soil. It was her goal to rescue every-one in her family, but Harriet would not bring along her husband, John, who had moved in with another woman.

Harriet now traveled twice each year, once in the spring and once during the autumn months. She brought enslaved people through ditches, swamps, mud heaps, shivering nights and humid hiding places. Once, Harriet and a group of freedom seekers had to cover themselves under heaps of cow droppings to stay out of sight. Even *that* didn't stop Harriet. She soon gained a reputation for being one of the most persistent conductors on the Underground Railroad. Harriet came to be known as the lady Moses, because, like the Bible's Moses, she led her people to freedom.

In the eyes of many White people who believed in slavery, Harriet was no kind of hero. They considered her a troublemaker who had to be stopped. They posted signs offering to pay anybody who spotted "the woman called Moses."

Harriet refused to let this dampen her spirit. Old Ben and Old Rit were still living on the Brodess plantation. Harriet had been waiting for the best time to rescue her parents so that they

were strong enough to make the trip. They were
now very old and frail, and she didn't want to wait
any longer. Making the long journey north would
require careful planning and plenty of time. On a
night in 1857, Harriet summoned her courage. She
found an old horse and crept onto the Brodess
property. With her bare hands, Harriet had built a
rickety wagon out of worn wood. She carefully
tucked her parents in the back and raced away.

The horse's hooves beat out a galloping rhythm. It was like a drumbeat anthem for Old Rit and Old Ben. Their strong daughter was successfully transporting them to freedom, with the help of others along the Underground Railroad!

Harriet had become so good at making escapes that her capture was now worth lots of money for anyone who could find and stop the woman called Moses.

Chapter 6

The Power of Progress

Harriet Tubman was unstoppable. She had fearlessly led countless people to freedom along the Underground Railroad for about ten years. She once said, "I never ran my train off the track, and I never lost a passenger."

Even when people encouraged Harriet to give up her work, she refused. Men warned Harriet that her life was in danger and that she was risking getting hurt, or even getting killed, being so bold. That was like telling a bird to stop flying because its wings might break or someone could shoot it down if it tried to fly too high. Harriet would keep reaching for the heights of the North Star's promise, no matter what others said. She didn't listen to anybody who didn't believe in the power of progress.

In 1861 when the Civil War broke out between America's Southern and Northern states, Harriet worked to help the Northern soldiers. The South believed Black people should stay enslaved forever. The North was fighting to end slavery. America was divided into two separate sides.

Many Black men enlisted in the Northern army to help the cause for freedom. Harriet served as a nurse for injured soldiers. She cleaned their

wounds and boiled root teas to help soothe diseases that gave them stomachaches.

On January 1, 1863, President Abraham Lincoln issued the Emancipation Proclamation, a document that called for the freedom of enslaved people who lived in certain parts of America. The proclamation didn't free everyone, and the war continued.

Harriet became a spy for the Northern army,

known as the Union, and worked under the command of Colonel James Montgomery. It would be Harriet's job to secretly get information from the Southern army, which was called the Confederacy.

At just a bit over five feet, she was the perfect size for spying. Harriet's height made her less noticeable in a group, especially when others around her were tall. With the knowledge she gained, Harriet could help the North win the war. Spying was dangerous. But danger never stopped Harriet.

The insider information Harriet gathered helped her lead the Union troops into enemy territory, allowing them to raid the Confederate army. This increased their chances of winning the war that would put an end to slavery.

Harriet was tough, gritty and brave. But it

was hard to do her work in the long skirts and lady-clothing she wore. Thankfully, Harriet heard about a woman named Amelia Bloomer who advocated for a "sensible costume for females." This outfit, called "bloomers," consisted of a small jacket and pants with a short skirt on top.

This "sensible" clothing was far from what people thought was proper or ladylike at that time. As a woman helping men fight a war, comfort and practicality made total sense.

Harriet said, "I made up my mind [that] I would never wear a long dress on an expedition . . . but would have a bloomer as soon as I could get one."

In April 1865 the Civil War ended. The North, the Union, had won the war. The Confederacy gave up its plans to form its own country and rejoined the Union as part of the United States of America. At the end of that year, in December, slavery was abolished. All people were free.

Harriet settled in Auburn, New York, with Old Rit and Old Ben. She created a nursing home for the elderly, but didn't earn enough money to support herself and her aging parents. Harriet requested that she be paid by the government for the work she had done during the Civil War as a nurse and spy. These wages were typically given to men after they had completed war service. Because Harriet's work wasn't recorded, everyone refused to pay her for the jobs she'd done in the past.

Harriet spoke up about this unfair treatment. She appealed to the federal government in 1865, and then again two years later. But still she was refused. Influential friends published articles in newspapers, telling why Harriet deserved the same money that was given to men who were war veterans.

Years before, Harriet had remarried a man named Nelson Davis, who had also served in the war. Nelson passed away in 1889. After he died, Harriet became eligible to receive a small amount of pension money as his widow. Harriet still pursued her own pension money, but continued to receive negative responses.

This went on for thirty-four years. Harriet did not give up! Finally, Harriet was granted an increase in the pension funds she received as the widow of a soldier. It was not enough to live on. She never received money for the work *she* did. This was hard on Harriet, but she stayed strong within herself. The time had come to tell her story so that future girls and women would be inspired to pursue their dreams and goals, even when others told them no.

Even though Harriet had never learned to read or write, her mind and memory were sharper than a batch of new pencils. She worked with a White woman named Sarah Bradford to tell her life story. It was a true tale of struggle, courage, resilience and victory, presented in the two books Sarah published, in 1869 and 1886, entitled *Harriet, Scenes in the Life of Harriet Tubman* and *Harriet Tubman: The Moses of Her People.*

Harriet's books became very popular, and are still read today. To encourage people to read her book, Harriet often gave speeches. She told people about her life and times. Harriet was a powerful

speaker who reminded her audiences that women are as strong and as smart as men. Harriet herself was living proof. She earned money for the books she wrote and the speeches she delivered.

She once said, "There was one of two things I had a right to, liberty or death; if I could not have one, I would have the other."

When Harriet died of pneumonia in 1913, government officials in Auburn, New York, placed a glistening bronze plaque on the front entrance of the Auburn Courthouse to honor her. It says, *She braved every danger and overcame every obstacle.*

Harriet's legacy can still be seen in the North Star's light. She inspired people when she once said, "I should fight for my liberty as long as my strength lasted." Harriet Tubman persisted by showing the world that the brightest stars shine forever.

HOW YOU CAN PERSIST

by Andrea Davis Pinkney

To honor Harriet Tubman's determination and bravery, here are some activities to enjoy with friends and family:

1. Help a lost person find their way.

2. Keep a journal about challenging situations you've come through. Make a list of what you did to succeed. Share this list with a friend in need.

3. Get a book about the constellations. Look for the North Star. Make a wish on its brilliance.

4. Honor the strength with which Harriet kept her family together by crafting a "legacy quilt." This can be done using "patches" created with family photos that express the important bonds between parents, sisters, brothers, elders and other relatives.

5. Listen to the words and melody of a traditional spiritual that may have been sung during Harriet's day. Talk about its meaning and how the powerful song inspires you today. Spirituals can be found online. They are often performed by choruses.

6. Host a "Harriet Happening," a gathering at which you and your friends celebrate Harriet Tubman's achievements. To do this, share books about Harriet. Recite her most notable quotes. Watch films about this freedom fighter. Talk about which traits of Harriet's mean the most to you, and why.

❡ References ❡

BOOKS

Bradford, Sarah H. *Harriet Tubman: The Moses of Her People*. Mineola, New York: Dover Publications, 2004.

———. *Scenes in the Life of Harriet Tubman*. Auburn, New York: W. J. Moses, 1869.

Clinton, Catherine. *Harriet Tubman: The Road to Freedom*. New York: Little, Brown, and Company, 2004.

Larson, Kate Clifford. *Bound for the Promised Land: Harriet Tubman, Portrait of an American Hero*. New York: Ballantine, 2004.

McDonough, Yona Zeldis. *Who Was Harriet Tubman?* New York: Penguin Workshop, 2002.

Pinkney, Andrea Davis. *Let It Shine: Stories of Black Women Freedom Fighters*. New York: Harcourt, Inc., 2000.

WEBSITES

NATIONAL WOMEN'S HISTORY MUSEUM

https://www.womenshistory.org/

   education-resources/biographies/

   harriet-tubman

NATIONAL PARK SERVICE

https://www.nps.gov/hatu/learn/historyculture/

   htubman.htm

HARRIETTUBMAN.ORG

http://www.harriet-tubman.org/category/

   biography/

http://www.harriet-tubman.org/quotes/

HARRIETTUBMANBIOGRAPHY.COM

http://www.harriettubmanbiography.com/
harriet-tubman-myths-and-facts.html

AMERICAN NATIONAL BIOGRAPHY

https://www.anb.org/view/10.1093/
anb/9780198606697.001.0001/
anb-9780198606697-e-1500707

ANDREA DAVIS PINKNEY is the *New York Times* bestselling and award-winning author of numerous books for children and young adults, and has been recognized by the Coretta Scott King Author Award committee with an honor for *Let It Shine: Stories of Black Women Freedom Fighters* and a medal for *Hand in Hand: Ten Black Men Who Changed America*. She is a four-time nominee for the NAACP Image Award, and has been inducted into the New York Writers Hall of Fame. In addition to her work as an author, Ms. Pinkney is a publishing executive. She has been named one of the "25 Most Influential Black Women in Business" by *The Network Journal*, and is among *Children's Health* magazine's "25 Most Influential People in Our Children's Lives."

Photo credit: *Christine Simmons*

You can visit Andrea Davis Pinkney online at
andreadavispinkney.com
and follow her on Twitter
@AndreaDavisPink

GILLIAN FLINT has worked as a professional illustrator since earning an animation and illustration degree in 2003. Her work has since been published in the UK, USA and Australia. In her spare time, Gillian enjoys reading, spending time with her family and puttering about in the garden on sunny days. She lives in the northwest of England.

You can visit Gillian Flint online at
gillianflint.com
or follow her on Twitter
@GillianFlint
and on Instagram
@gillianflint_illustration

CHELSEA CLINTON is the author of the #1 *New York Times* bestseller *She Persisted: 13 American Women Who Changed the World*; *She Persisted Around the World: 13 Women Who Changed History*; *She Persisted in Sports: American Olympians Who Changed the Game*; *Don't Let Them Disappear: 12 Endangered Species Across the Globe*; *It's Your World: Get Informed, Get Inspired & Get Going!*; *Start Now!: You Can Make a Difference*; with Hillary Clinton, *Grandma's Gardens* and *Gutsy Women*; and, with Devi Sridhar, *Governing Global Health: Who Runs the World and Why?* She is also the Vice Chair of the Clinton Foundation, where she works on many initiatives, including those that help empower the next generation of leaders. She lives in New York City with her husband, Marc, their children and their dog, Soren.

You can follow Chelsea Clinton on Twitter
@ChelseaClinton
or on Facebook at
facebook.com/chelseaclinton

ALEXANDRA BOIGER has illustrated nearly twenty picture books, including the She Persisted books by Chelsea Clinton; the popular Tallulah series by Marilyn Singer; and the Max and Marla books, which she also wrote. Originally from Munich, Germany, she now lives outside of San Francisco, California, with her husband, Andrea, daughter, Vanessa, and two cats, Luiso and Winter.

You can visit Alexandra Boiger online at
alexandraboiger.com
on follow her on Instagram
@alexandra_boiger

Don't miss the rest of the books in the

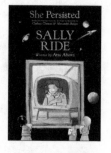

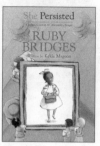

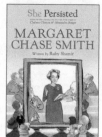

She Persisted series!

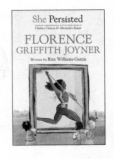

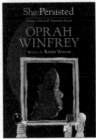

ACKNOWLEDGMENTS

The most persistent women I know often remind me that strength comes from not going it alone. This is especially true in bookmaking, which requires many persistent hands to bring stories to young people. I would like to thank the following mighty women, members of the "Persisterhood" who made this book possible. Publisher Jill Santopolo and editor Talia Benamy, thank you for your persistent, keen, and brilliant editorial direction in helping me tell Harriet Tubman's story. Alexandra Boiger, you have persisted in creating beautiful covers for so many books, including this one. Gillian Flint, thank you for your beautiful renderings of Harriet Tubman's journey to freedom that are depicted on the interior pages. Lisa Von Drasek, Librarian/Curator, University of Minnesota, Children's Literature Research Collections, thank you for your persistence in preserving the importance of children's literature. Rebecca Sherman, my agent, gratitude abounds for being persistent in your guidance and good orderly direction.

Historians and authors Catherine Clinton and Kate Clifford Larson, I appreciate your comprehensive writings about Harriet Tubman that served as invaluable research material that enabled me to be persistent as I confirmed facts, figures, dates, and names. Chelsea Clinton, thank you for persisting in your ongoing mission of reaching young people through the powerful stories of women who, like Harriet Tubman herself, offer a North Star to all children. Chloe Pinkney, my daughter, immense gratitude to you for providing invaluable feedback during the creation of this book. You inspire me with your beautiful persistence. And last but certainly not least, Brian Pinkney, my husband, while you are not an official member of the Persisterhood of women, thank you for your persistence in loving me and letting me love you!